Psalms In my palms
Vol. 2

I0445514

Poetry, Prayer, and Pages for Your Soul

By

Coolgmack

Published in the United States.
Cover design and layout by Coolgmack
ISBN: 979-8-9930046-4-8
Contact/Website: Coolgmack.com   coolgmack@gmail.com
@coolgmack on all platforms

Dedication to Freedom

To God, my ultimate Deliverer, I offer this truth: I was once cuffed to a pen, my lonely best friend, yet now I am equipped with a purpose that transcends the prison walls. I thank the incredible fans who believe in this profound transformation, and even my old friends, for the clear contrast between who I was and the man I've become proves I've come a long way. Thank You, Lord, for saving me time after time, every time the enemy tried to claim my life and labor. I was not myself; I was possessed by the dust demon, and I am eternally grateful to my family who held me down, knowing my crazy ways weren't the real me. Thank you, God, for this chance to be great again, because though I am not yet free physically, my mind is completely liberated. Thank you to all my people whose tongue-swords sharpen my resolve and keep me on the right path. I extend my deep gratitude to Union Baptist and John Jenkins, and a heartfelt R.I.P. to Paul Sheppard. Your sermons carried me through the toughest times, and your words continue to guide my freedom.

Chapter 1: Morning and Purpose

Morning Prayer of Purpose

Morning breaks—no time for yawning,
I'm not tired, I'm wired for the dawning.
Called to pursue what the Lord requires,
To lift my life to a standard much higher.
First, I bow to God, the ultimate Sire,
The One above all, numero uno entire.

Today unfolds another sacred chance
To rise above my unfortunate circumstances,
To embrace the higher stakes, I seek,
To find strength when I am weak.

God willing—may my faith remain,
May it never fail or cause me pain,
May it keep my mental state aligned,
A steady anchor for my heart and mind.

For all it takes is to trust in He who reigns,
And honest work through losses and through pain,
To receive the blessings heaven sends
A grace that heals, restores, and mends.

And when those blessings fill your hands,
Remember God who understands,
Don't forget from whom ye came,
Share your testament, proclaim His name.
May your day be wonderful and true,
May it be productive through and through,
And remember it's always right to pray
When you need His love to light your way.

"Before turning the page, take a few moments to reflect. Write down prayers, thoughts, or insights stirred in your heart. Let this page hold your conversation with God."

Ezekiel seen Jesus coming

In the twenty-fifth year of captivity's chain,
Ezekiel sat in exile, bearing burden and pain,
January tenth marked the day, cold and clear,
Fourteen winters since his city fell, year after year.

Then it hit—a vision or was it a dream?
So vivid, so holy, realer than it seemed,
From God Himself, the Most High, the Supreme,
A revelation descended like a celestial beam.

He was carried away from Israel's troubled ground,
Lifted by divine hands without a sound,
Set upon a mountain peak, lofty and profound,
Where halos of Gabriel did shimmer all around.

Toward the south, his spirit-eyes could see
The structure of a city in sacred geometry,
Every wall, every gate ordained to be
A dwelling place of glory, of eternity.

God's Spirit took him there—make no mistake,
This was no ordinary journey, for a prophet's sake,
And behold! A man stood there, awake,
A brown-skinned guardian, solid, not opaque.

With the appearance of bronze, radiant and bright,

Like LeBron, he stood tall in the holy light,
His kingdom was his glory, a magnificent sight,
Those who witnessed stood appalled at his might.

In his hands: a line of flax, both humble and divine
A fiber for sustenance, for textiles fine,
For sheets of covering, a sacred sign,
And a measuring rod, perfectly aligned.

He stood as an image of God, chosen and known,
His presence in the gateway, set in stone,
Unbroken by the world, unmoved, alone,
And from his lips came words in a holy tone:

"Son of man, look with your eyes!" he cried.
"Hear with your ears, let nothing hide!
Fix your mind on everything I show inside,
For what's clear is revealed, nothing denied!"
The rest unfolds as history—or is it His story?
Either way, it's written in eternal glory,
Not a mystery, just facts, that's mandatory,
Divine Truth, an ancient proven story

So, remember Ezekiel's vision on that sacred day,
When God pulled back the veil to display,
The blueprint of heaven in earthly array,
And called His prophet to see, to hear, and to obey.
So, let's pray!

Faith in Motion

I've come a long way
From who I used to be,
Still fighting demons
Only God and I can see.
The pain tried to break me,
The world tried to shake me,
But through every trial,
My faith remade me.

I learned slowly

"Before turning the page, take a few moments to reflect. Write down prayers, thoughts, or insights stirred in your heart. Let this page hold your conversation with God."

Holy Thread

All things shall weave a holy song,
Though paths seem twisted, dark, and long.
The hands of God shape every thread,
And lead His children where He's led.

The storm may roar, the night may fall,
Yet He is sovereign over all.
When men intend to bring to despair,
God bends to bless with tender care.

The loss, the wound, the breaking years,
He gathers up our prayers and tears.
And in His love, no pain is vain,
For grace will bloom from grief and strain.

For those who love Him, our hearts aligned,
Our steps are guided, soul and mind.
"The cross once seemed like death's domain,
Yet from its weight sprang endless gain."

So trust the plan you cannot see,
For God works for good eternally.
His purpose stands, His Word is true,
And all things work together for good—for you.

"Before turning the page, take a few moments to reflect. Write down prayers, thoughts, or insights stirred in your heart. Let this page hold your conversation with God."

A Prayer of Trust in God's Plan

Heavenly Father, When my path feels twisted, dark, and long, you remind me that You are weaving it into a holy song. Your hands shape every thread of my life, and though I may not see the pattern, I trust Your design. For You, I will make that sacrifice. When storms roar and nights grow cold, help me remember Lord, that You are sovereign over all. What others intend for harm, You bend for good. As I remember you in those dark times like I should. You turn my despair into strength, my pain into purpose. you gather my tears, Lord, and hear my prayers. I know that You are near and Your spirit is working. "Let no wound be wasted, no strain be in vain. Bloom Your grace from grief, and let me see Your mercy as the light that guides me through pain." Lord, teach me to trust the plan that I cannot see. Help me trust the process and not get impatient or antsy. Please align my heart with Yours, my steps with Your will. For even the cross I bear was once a symbol of death but still became the symbol of a doorway to eternal life and endless love.

Father, help me walk in faith, not by my human sight, believing that all things work together for good, for those who love You and are called according to Your purpose.

In Jesus' name I pray,
Amen.

"Before turning the page, take a few moments to reflect. Write down prayers, thoughts, or insights stirred in your heart. Let this page hold your conversation with God."

Chapter 2: Repentance and Redemption

A Sinner's Plea: Prayer for Forgiveness and Protection

God, please forgive me for what I'm about to do,
I came before You broke, lost, and confused.
About to commit wrongs I know aren't right,
But I'm desperate, Lord, stumbling through this night.

I'm just a prodigal son, a product of my place,
Born into struggle, trying to find your grace,
Please protect me from the man-made disease,
The systems that bring us all to our knees.
Don't let their poison cause me to dis-ease,
Don't let their sickness infect me, please,
Don't let them inject me with disorders they conceived.
With labels and traps designed to make us grieve.

Lord, please see my heart—it's good, I swear,
My intentions are pure beneath this despair,
It's just so hard to get a start in here,
In this world where everything costs more each year.
The weight is exceedingly too expensive to bear,
And it's leading me to sin—I'm painfully aware,

I'll accept my consequences when they come due,
But I'm hoping, praying, that I'm forgiven by You.
"I promise, Lord—this is the final run,

After this last sale, I'll be done.
I'll quit, I swear, no more grime
I'll walk away clean from this life of crime."
I come to You because I'm powerless here.
Over my predicament, my poverty, and my fear,
Please make it make sense, help me understand,
I need Your benediction, Lord—hold my hand.
Guide me through this darkness I'm walking through,
Give me strength to do what I need to do,
And when it's over, help me find my way,
Back to righteousness, back to You, I pray.

In Your mercy, Lord. Amen.

A Prayer for Protection and Faith

Father, thank You that You know every hardship and hurt. Every unfair and difficult situation I have faced. You know all the times I was oppressed and even arrested for unjust reasons... Still, it's You that I believe in. I choose to believe that You have more blessings and favor for me than I can even dream of. I trust that You will protect me—from my inner me and from my unknown enemies. I believe that I have come under Your wings, and that no sudden lie or scheme will prosper against me.

In Jesus' Name I pray,

Amen.

"Before turning the page, take a few moments to reflect. Write down prayers, thoughts, or insights stirred in your heart. Let this page hold your conversation with God."

Accept Responsibility

Lord, I will accept responsibility for my actions.
I can't blame anyone else for the choices I made.
I was busy chasing instant satisfaction
Now I have to accept the consequences
that came my way.

No more doing things
that leads to the wrong route
Like putting that blunt to my mouth,
My lips on his spouse,
Or that gun in that house.

I know the legacy was stolen,
Now I'm owning my history dismay.
Holding myself accountable.
With my life, I played—now I have to pay.

God is just;
He knows how to bring me back to the path.
In cuffs...
So, I wasn't arrested. I was rescued from His wrath.
Every day I prayed and revered, confessing to Him.
God is majestic; He plans with perfection.

Any father disciplines his child
to teach them their lessons.
Thank God for this discipline
The kind that turns kids into men.

I accept my chastisement
And the blessings that come
From learning through them.
Whether you're a Muslim or a born-again Christian,
God will heal you of your sins and afflictions.

So I'm confident in the Lord,
Because it's obvious what I'm here for.
I'm humbled and grateful for His sake.
God is so good, God is great.
One hand washes the other.
Both hands wash the face.

Prayer of Accountability and Restoration

Lord, I come before You with a humble heart,
Ready to accept responsibility from the start.
For every choice I made, every path I took,
I can't blame anyone — I wrote my own book.

I was busy chasing instant satisfaction,
living for the moment.
Now I must accept the consequences
and pray for atonement.

No more will I be doing things I know are wrong,
No more singing that destructive song.
Through Jesus, my life has been restored,
holding myself accountable for all I've done.

God, You are just, and You know the way
To bring me back to the righteous ways
Every day I prayed, every night I confessed,
Revering Your name, seeking Your rest.

God, You are majestic — Your plans are perfected,
Every step I take is in Your divine direction.

Now I'm in a position to obey and listen,
to walk in Your light, and let my life glisten.

I accept my chastisement and all I must learn,
the benefits of Your fire — the refining burn.
I'm humbled and grateful for Your mercy and care.
God, You are so good beyond compare.

God, You are great — Your love never cease.
Teach me to help others as You've helped me,
To lift up my brothers so they too can be free.
Thank You for saving me, for pulling me
My life is no longer mine — it belongs to thee

In Your holy name, with gratitude and surrender. Amen.

A Prayer for Protection and Guidance

I hope You hear me,
I hope You protect me and stay near me.
I hope You're watching over me,
I hope You show me your favor endlessly.
I'm taking care of myself and my neighbor,
Helping others out, doing good labor.
I'm protecting the weak, lifting the meek,
I pray day and night before I sleep.
I read my sacred books — I understand,
I'm doing the best I can with what's in my hand.
God, please watch over me and love me.
Please protect me and my family.
Shield us from the oppressors
Those with power and wealth,
Grant us justice, mercy, and health.
Dear God, dear God—please help me!
Guide my heart, my path, my destiny.

"Before turning the page, take a few moments to reflect. Write down prayers, thoughts, or insights stirred in your heart. Let this page hold your conversation with God."

Chapter 3: Faith in Adversity

Perseverance Terrence

Slow progress is better than no progress
You gotta keep going through the nonsense
and get beyond it.
You must be honest with yourself,
And find the strength that's within you
Even when no one else wanna help,
You must continue.

Things will get thrown at you,
And it'll feel like the world's against you
But all you need is the Almighty G-O-D to defend
you.
"You might feel your back pressed to the wall,
But that's when you rise and stand tall.
Pick yourself up—don't let yourself stall."

Especially when it's hard to foresee opportunity
That's when you gotta believe,
And pray out your impurities.
It helps to have blind faith and a positive mind state,
To find that gr8 that lies inside of you
But you gotta be awake.
If you sleep, Satan will lie to you,
Connive you and supply you with false revelations.

28

"He plants premonitions for premeditation

If you don't seek spiritual education,
You'll be fed lies and mental contamination."

He'll send garbage straight into your cerebrum
What you put in is what you get out.
Knowledge is the key to your mental freedom.
Wisdom water that drought
You can stay numb, or strive to make a change
Admitting you have a problem
Is the first step to break the chains.

Galatians 6:9 (NIV)
"Let us not become weary in doing good,
for at the proper time we will reap a harvest if we do not
give up."

Spirituality in environments where there's no hospitality

Be honest with God and yourself. Ask for help. Follow these steps and you will find strength in confinement or when you're faced with hostile environments. Whether it's jail, prison, or the penitentiary, remember to put God first. Then remember faith without works = dirt. Practicing spirituality in confinement and hostile environments. These steps are meant for you to find strength and faith when faced with adversity. I know it hurts to be away from your family. So, use these steps to overcome fear, anxiety and insanity. These steps are meant to be practical not radical. Practice these steps to clean your soul.

#1. Pray daily! Start and end your day with a prayer as soon as you wake up. Give God thanks just for the sake of waking up.

#2. Read your religion or spiritual books. Knowledge is power. Wisdom is putting it to use. Understanding is the best part of being alive in your spiritual pursuits.

#3. Get acquainted with meditation... spend quality time in reflecting on a better way and focusing on God's greatness.

#4. Is finding fellowship. Finding brothers who share your faith and beliefs. You could study together and encourage each other through the grief. Uplift and support each sister and brother remember this too shall pass. Hopefully it's brief.

#5. Is showing love just for the sake of the lord, even though times can be rough or you get bored. Still be kind and respectful, never neglectful to everyone including those that ridicule, show favor. Learn to forgive sooner than later. Let grudges go even show love to your haters because God is greater!

#6. Maintain your integrity, morals, and principles. Stay true to your values and still be an individual. Avoid gangs, cliques, and negative influences. Be cautious who you break bread with.

#7. Use your time wisely. You can either be a student or a fool. Do your time, don't let the time do you! Read, study or maybe learn a new skill. Because idleness kills! Strive to have personal growth. Use creative expressions that are real. Engage in activities like poetry or maybe getting a degree that can pay the bills.

#8. Exercise daily! Physically and mentally. Keep your body healthy. Try not to stress. Some things are just meant to be. Eat the right foods. It's better to be fit than to be wealthy.

#9. Stay cool, calm, and collectively. Respond with grace even when faced with hostility... respectfully.

#10. Endure all with faith. Be honest and trust in God's process to get beyond this.
This won't last forever... Take these jewels and put them on your crown to help you get past whatever hostile environment you're in.

Behold, Lord

Behold, Lord, how much more
Shall I suffer in this somber slumber?
Every other day I wonder if I'll live to see another.
I just saw my next-door neighbor get cut up.
Lord, please protect me,
From these rapists and bloodsuckers.
They want to prosecute me because of what I believe:
that Jesus was the Son of God, just like me, respectfully.
Most of us are born with the same brain capacity
but only 5% of the world uses its full potential, actually
They laugh at me, they harass me, try to stab at me
because I prostrate 5 times a day emphatically.
But I was created for His purpose, in God's image
which I gladly and earnestly repent for my sins.
I am undeserving.
The grace of God returns it to Him
Because He thinks that I'm worth it,
but I'm far from perfect.
I made a lot of mistakes
Those lessons I learned with.
I apply my faith and works in my worship,
For I know You long to save me
from my oppressors who are so cruel.
They lock me in a cell, Two cold rations
barely enough to chew.

Lord, I'm sorry.
Forgive me for taking my freedom for granted.
I should have watered the seeds that You planted.
Now I'm back in this same state
Where Your lessons were abandoned,
stranded in this familiar place where I'm remanded.
My faith is the same but aged in the face.
Twenty years later, still making the same mistakes.
Please don't let this be my fate.
I'm so sick and tired of trying to do it my way.
Not thinking I had a problem
Were the problems that I faced.
I was weak, enslaved by my addiction.
Lord Almighty, please forgive my affliction.
Give me the benefit of the doubt.
They got me cellies with a mouse.
God help me out.
No hot water coming out the sink.
Just cats running their mouths,
Disturbing my sleep at night, I can't think
Yelling and screaming like they're possessed
By Antichrist and the demons.
Every night I read and prayed for forgiveness
And repented.
Hopefully soon the Lord will come through and end this.
I'm far from innocent.
I'm a sinner that sinned and deserves my punishments
Again, and again.

Just please give me another chance
To worship Your name.
Let me be the testament of Your purpose and aim.
What good would my talents do
If they're buried in prison?
Give me a chance to advance
And enlighten Your children,
for I am just one of Your prodigal sons
That went astray off the straight path.
It was only logical for me to return.
I put my past in the past
Everything happens for a reason.
Or for a season
Tough times or cataclysms, He will never leave you,
if you just believe in Him.

So I know that this, too, shall pass,
and that You never let me face a burden
That I can't grasp.
I'm confident that You, my God,
Will come and save me.
I will continue to pray to You
and praise You daily.

Even though now it's dark,
I see the light at the end of the tunnel.
The Truth will set me free.
God, I love You.

"Before turning the page, take a few moments to reflect. Write down prayers, thoughts, or insights stirred in your heart. Let this page hold your conversation with God."

Season of Faith

Don't judge your life by winter's bitter cold,
When frost obscures the story yet untold.
One season's pain, one chapter's sharp dismay
Cannot define the fullness of your days.

You cannot see what God sees from above
The masterpiece He's weaving out of love.
So let it unfold, release your tight-held grip,
And trust the potter's hand that will not slip.

The puzzle pieces scattered all over the floor
Make sense to Him, who knows what lies in store.
You did what's right, yet wrong crashed through
But God is still in control of all that you do.

What looks like setback in your weary eyes
Is a setup for the comeback in disguise.
Positioning you now for something new,
Fresh levels of destiny are breaking through.

You'll see His hand move mountains and trees
That you can't see,
Orchestrating miracles-to-be.
Like David, you can rest in this—it's true:
Your future's set in hands that fashioned you.

So quit your worrying about tomorrow's woes
Your destiny is sealed, your fortune's gold.
He's lined up good breaks waiting down the road.
The right people to lighten up the heavy loads.

Solutions to the problems that you face
Already worked out by His perfect grace.
All part of His divine and His holy plans
Come back to peace, dear child, take His hand.

He didn't bring you here to let you fall,
His path is clear, won't steer you wrong
What He has started, He will see complete,
Your journey rests secure beneath His feet.

Chapter 4: Renewal and Transformation

Rising Above It All: Prayer

Father, thank You that it's possible to rise above even the hardest trials and painful situations. Thank You that I can walk in integrity, and that bitterness and anger won't get the best of me. I choose to keep honoring You, to stay steady, strong, and true.

I will not let one offense take root in my heart, nor let resentment tear me apart.

When I'm tempted to give in or run away, I need you to remind me, Lord, You are my rock that won't break. Help me to forgive, to release, to let go. To trust that You're working in ways I don't know. Give me peace beyond what eyes can see, and joy that lifts me from this misery sea. Thank You that Your mercy renews each day. Your love never falters; it shows me the righteous way. I choose to keep walking, humble and pure. For with You, Father, I am secure.
In Jesus' name, Amen.

"Before turning the page, take a few moments to reflect. Write down prayers, thoughts, or insights stirred in your heart. Let this page hold your conversation with God."

A Prayer to Carry

When storms arise and shadows fall,
You are the strength that steadies all.
When doubt and fear clouds my heart and mind,
Your mercy comes, so pure, so kind.
You lift me up when my spirit breaks,
You calm the sea, and my soul awakes.
In every trial, great or small,
Your grace remains, surpassing all.
When friends depart and hope seems gone,
Your presence stays, your anchor's strong.
You teach my heart to rest and wait,
for every blessing comes in faith.
Forgive my faults, renew my ways,
and let my every breath become Your praise.

Though I may stumble, I will endure,
for in Your Word, my path is sure.
Let love be planted deep within,
that I may serve through losses and wins.
And when this journey finds its end,
Receive me, Lord—my God, my all, my Friend.
Father, You know best in all I seek,
You guide my steps when I am tired and weak.
Through mysteries I cannot understand,
my life remains secure within Your hand.
You alone are God, my faith stands sure

"Before turning the page, take a few moments to reflect. Write down prayers, thoughts, or insights stirred in your heart. Let this page hold your conversation with God."

The Rock at the Bottom

God granted my life a revival
When I finally committed myself to Him.
I picked up the Bible
And it became my tool for survival.
I had to learn to have faith,
to believe in Him—not in idols.
I shall not sell my soul to my rival,
Nor for money, money—no bill idol.

Now I don't even walk the same way,
Or talk the same way.
My spirit was renewed.
But for that to happen,
My old ways had to be subdued.
I was used and abused by the devil,
Digging my own grave
With him providing the shovel.
I used to sin with my eyes, but I had to let that go.

No longer could Satan pump me full of poison.
He used to taunt me, harass me,
Try to get me to do his deeds — to join in.
Actually, he was constantly after me.
The spiritual warfare was raging within me.
I needed God to send His messages
Through pastor messengers to reach me

And He did. He spoke through Union Baptist.
Then something magical happened — something holy.
I was filled with the Holy Ghost.
But this wasn't just a boast or a hoax
I took off my coat and stepped into the truth.
Shortly after, I started praising Him. Amen.
And then, soon after,
I started getting attacked by Satan.
I was saved, but still a baby in faith.
And Satan took advantage.
My world caved in.

He knows how to come in your favorite flavors.
Mine were drugs and women,
And promiscuous behaviors.
I had to hit my head on rock bottom
Just so God could show me
He was the rock at the bottom.
Without Him as my foundation,
I would've drowned in Satan's basin.
It's like building a house on sand
As soon as the storm comes, it shifts.
That's not in God's plan.
In His grip, you won't slip

My God is not a God
Who wants me living in defeat,
but standing on my feet, walking to His beat.

It's Him that gets my glory.

And I'm getting ready

Ready for the restoration that's coming for me.

It's promised to me,

As long as I repent and honor Him.

And repent from my sins

Thank You, Lord, for saving me, for embracing me.

When they wanted to deflate and erase me,

You changed me gracefully.

You gave me mercy.

You faithfully protected me

When my enemies wanted to hurt me.

And for that — I praise You, Almighty God.

Worthy, holy, and forever true...

All the glory belongs to You.

Matthew 7:24–25

[24] "Therefore everyone who hears these words of mine and puts them into practice is like a wise man who built his house on the rock. [25] The rain came down, the streams rose, and the winds blew and beat against that house; yet it did not fall, because it had its foundation on the rock.

"Before turning the page, take a few moments to reflect. Write down prayers, thoughts, or insights stirred in your heart. Let this page hold your conversation with God."

Divine Design

After the storm, came peace and stillness.
God calmed my soul and granted me forgiveness.
I learned that freedom isn't just the absence of chains;
It's the renewal of the mind, the cleansing of pain.
He took the guilt that haunted me at night
And turned my darkness into light.
I started seeing purpose in every scar,
Realizing I had drifted really far
And how near He truly was.

No more living halfway—I am all in.
Temptation still knocks, but I refused to let it in.
The same hands that once reached for sin
Now reach in prayer again and again.
I learned obedience through the fire,
Patience through the waiting,
gratitude through the suffering.
The devil was a liar.
Each trial became a teacher;
Each loss became a seed for deeper faith.
I saw how God can turn a cell into a sanctuary,
How He can take your pain and make it praise-worthy.
He showed me that He doesn't run out of mercy
Every time I fell, He lifted me higher.
Every time I doubted, He proved Himself faithful.
every time I questioned His timing,

He reminded me that delay is not denial...
It's divine designing.
Now I walk not by sight, but by faith.
I carry peace where pride once stayed.
The same mouth that cursed now bless;
The same mind that wandered now rests.
I'm no longer the man I used to be...
I'm becoming the one He called me to be.
My past doesn't define me;
His promise refines me.
And though the battle isn't over,
I fight differently now
not with fear, but with faith.
with strength, not with doubt.
For I know my Redeemer lives,
I know His grace forgives,
And I know that what He started in me,
He will finish completely.
So I keep pressing on, walking to His beat,
Because I've learned that real strength
Is standing in surrender at His feet.

Praise be to the Lord
the Rock at the bottom and the Glory at the top.
Now I stand, not as who I was,
but as proof of what God does for His flock.
He took my pain
and turned it into purpose,

My failures into faith,
My shame into service.
I once walked in chains, now I walk in grace.
Every scar on my soul has found its place.
Not as a reminder of defeat,
But as a testimony that God never leaves.
He didn't just save me to sit still;
He called me to climb the hill,
To tell the broken that healing is real,
To remind the lost that Jesus still heals.

So I speak with fire now, but it's not my own.
It's the Spirit of God that sets the tone.

Every word I breathe, every tear I cry,
Is a seed He waters from up high.
I reach for those still drowning in sin,
because I know what it's like to need rescuing within.
I've seen the devil's traps, the world's disguise,
But I've also seen victory through heaven's eyes.

So I carry the light into the darkest places,
Telling the hopeless there's still salvation.
If He can reach me, He can reach you too.
If He can change me, He can make all things new.

Now I mentor the broken, I pray for the lost,
I speak to the hurting about the cross

Not because I'm perfect, I'm far from that,
But because I serve a God who brought me back.

He gave me vision when I had none,
He gave me strength when I was done,
He gave me courage to keep walking
when I wanted to run.

My story is not tragedy—it's triumph.
It's not defeat—it's deliverance.
It's not shame—it's salvation.
It's the evidence that His grace still reigns.

So I'll keep spreading His Word, loud and clear,
To every ear that's willing to hear.
From the pulpit to the promise, I've been restored.
I was once broken—but now I'm reborn.

To God be the glory, forever and true,
For every breath, every blessing,
And every soul He leads me to.

Equipped for Destiny

My Lord and Father, I come before You today with a heart full of gratitude. Thank You that I am not confined by the whispers of those around me or their attitudes. Nor am I shaken by their opinions. Their words, whether meant to praise me or to criticize me, do not define me. I am grateful that You have set my path and given me the tools and strength to walk it. You have strengthened me for the purpose You have set before me. I am equipped. I will not let the voices of the world distract me from the sound of Your call. I will not allow the doubts and fears of others to become a trap for my fall. You have placed in my heart. The destiny You have written for me is not subjected to the opinions of man. I close my ears to the discouraging words and open my spirit to Your empowering truth. I now understand. I stand firm on the promise that what You have started, You will also complete. My confidence is not weak or based on my own ability but in Your divine power working through me.

Therefore, I declare today that I will not be swayed. I will not be intimidated. For in Christ, I was saved. I will run the race You have set before me with perseverance and courage. Let my life be a testament to Your faithfulness as I flourish. Let me be a reflection of Your unfailing love. In the mighty and precious name of Jesus, Amen.

"Before turning the page, take a few moments to reflect. Write down prayers, thoughts, or insights stirred in your heart. Let this page hold your conversation with God."

Remember Who You Are

When others fail to lift your head,
And words of doubt are spread instead,
Remember this, my brother, take heed:
You have within you all you need.

Though they may not your worth proclaim,
Call on your Father's Holy Name.
For God does see what they don't see;
He sees the crown He placed on thee.

You are a Child of God Most High,
Beneath His watchful, loving eye.
With favor's grace upon your brow,
Remember who you are right now.
You are unique, no one the same,
A masterpiece He chose to frame.
Let this deep truth within you stay,
And light your spirit every day.

Take a pen in your hand, let words now flow,
And tell the world the truth you know:
Who you are in Christ, the surest part,
A living promise inside your heart.

"Before turning the page, take a few moments to reflect. Write down prayers, thoughts, or insights stirred in your heart. Let this page hold your conversation with God."

The Whisper

We wait for thunder from the sky,
for Moses' mountain, burning high,
for voices crashing through the clouds
God's glory is brilliant, bold, and loud.

But listen closer, bend your ear:
He speaks in whispers that we can hear,
a gentle stirring in the soul,
a quiet truth that makes us whole.

Not forceful winds or earthquake's roar,
but impressions at the heart's own door
a prompting soft, a sudden knowing,
the Spirit's voice, persistent, flowing.

Six times the Savior said to those
who walked with Him through dusty roads:
"Let those with ears now hear!" He cried,
inviting us to step inside.

And seven times in Revelation,
He adds this sacred invitation:
"Hear what the Spirit has to say"
He's speaking still, this very day.

Your inner ears were meant to find

these whispers of the Divine Mind,
these gentle tugs upon your heart,
These promptings meant to set you apart.
It's easy, though, to turn away,
to drown His voice in noise and fray,
to push it down, ignore the call,
pretend we never heard it at all.

But if you listen, if you obey
these gentle whispers day by day,
these small suggestions from above,
these quiet words of the perfect love

God will guide you, step by step,
through every promise He has kept,
down paths you never knew were there,
the best roads found through whispered prayer.

So, tune your heart, be still, be near
The gentle voice is always here.

Prayer of Confidence in God

Dear Heavenly Father, I thank You today,
For shaping my life in Your wonderful ways.
You planted great seeds of purpose in me,
A vessel of promise, created to be.

You live deep within; Your Spirit's my guide,
In You, I find strength, no need to hide.
Your love is my anchor, Your truth is my song,
With You by my side, I know I belong.

I won't chase the praise or the words of the crowd,
For Your gentle whisper speaks love out loud.
I'm made in Your image, perfectly whole,
Your handpicked creation—body and soul.

I'm sufficient in You, my heart is at rest,
For You are my portion, my all, my best.
I'll walk with my head held high every day,
In Jesus' Name, I humbly pray. Amen.

"Before turning the page, take a few moments to reflect. Write down prayers, thoughts, or insights stirred in your heart. Let this page hold your conversation with God."

Greater Is He.

Today, I declare I'm equipped and empowered,
Anointed for purpose at this very hour.
God called me forth, and I answered the call,
My worth flows from Him, the Giver of all.

No longer seeking what people approve,
I'm anchored in Him, no need to prove.
I'm Created His image, handpicked for His plan.
Strong, healthy, favored—this is who I am.

The forces with me tower over mountains high,
Greater than anything that the world may try.
I stand in His promise, I walk in His light,
Blessed and beloved, equipped for the fight.

My steps are ordered, my paths are made clear,
Divine assigned replaces all fear.
Each breath I take is a gift from above,
Sustained and surrounded by infinite love.

The enemy trembles when I speak His name,
For greater is He who ignites this flame.
No weapon formed against me shall stand,
I'm sealed and protected by His mighty hand.

.

I rise with purpose, I move with grace,
Reflecting the glory that shines from His face.
My words carry power, my faith moves the hill,
I'm walking in freedom, surrendering to His will.

Today and forever, this truth I proclaim:
I'm chosen, I'm worthy, redeemed by His name.
Anointed and empowered to fulfill my call,
In Him, I am everything—He is my all.

1 John 4:4
New International Version
4 You, dear children, are from God and have overcome them, because the one who is in you is greater than the one who is in the world.

Trust the Process for Success

How we wait for God's promises — that's up to us.
We have to trust His process if we want success.
You can sit there discouraged, asking,
"God, when's it my turn?"
"God, why me? Why do these lessons burn?"
"God, why can't I lose weight, can't this problem fade?"
Like it's magic—we want blessings on demand, pre-paid.

But faith doesn't work that way.
You can't rush what He's arranging.
You gotta let Him happen,
Because His timing's never changing.

Be a believer, not a doubter,
Let His plan go into action.
Keep honoring God — that's your chain reaction.

When you keep praising, not complaining,
Giving Him glory, not fainting,
you'll change the narrative of your story,
And step into blessings made for your testimony.
God will bless you accordingly.
You'll see moments unfold
that only God could make happen
That's a fact!
No fiction, no fractions.

It's the hand of God that defies the odds,
That makes a way when the doors are locked.
He moves the mountains, parts the seas,
Open paths you thought would never be.
So stay in peace.
Pray and release.

You have got the most powerful force in the universe on your side.
You got His power in you, in your heart He resides.
It's strong, it's blazing, it's true.
It's powerful.
It's amazing.
It's yours.

In the name of Jesus Christ, amen

A Prayer of Unwavering Faith

Father, thank You! That You are my God, and that alone, that sacred truth, is reason enough, more than enough, to never settle in the shallows, to never waver in the waivers of unbelieving hearts.

Thank You for another day, this gift of breath, this morning grace. Thank You for relieving burdens, for lifting problems from my shoulders, for showing me Your faithful hand.

Thank You that my faith can grow, can stretch and strengthen, rise and glow, becoming fully persuaded in the magnitude of Your power— the power that spoke worlds into being, the power that raises the dead, the power that keeps every promise. I am going to keep believing, even when the wait grows long. I am going to keep praising, even before I see the answer. I am going to keep receiving with open hands and a grateful heart. I am going to keep claiming the promises You've spoken over me. I honor You for what is here, for blessings present, seen, and known. I honor You for what's on the way in, for promises still traveling toward me, for gifts wrapped in Your perfect timing, for answered prayers already released from heaven's throne.
You are faithful. You are good. You are God.
In Jesus' Name, Amen.

"Before turning the page, take a few moments to reflect. Write down prayers, thoughts, or insights stirred in your heart. Let this page hold your conversation with God."

Chapter 5: The Word and Wisdom

Macpsalm 37.1 Do Not Be Afraid

Do not be afraid of the wicked,
Do not be envious of the people who do you wrong.
They will soon fade in the stenches,
And will be blown away like sand in a storm.

Miracles God has shown today
To trust in His creed,
Repent your sinful ways,
And do good deeds.

So you will live in peace,
And take delight in the Lord who is our Sire.
Enjoy His security
He will give us all that our hearts desire.

Commit your ways to the Lord,
And for you, He will act.
Trust in Him every day
For everyday He has made, that's a fact.

He will make our vindications shine so bright,
And the justice of our causes will be brought to life.
Be still before the Lord and wait patiently for Him.
Don't be afraid of those who prosper
in their own mayhem,

Or those that kill who have forsaken Him
For them, too shall see their day. Amen.
Refrain from anger, and turn away from sin,
Do not fret or be afraid
It only leads to evilness within.

For sure, the wicked and vicious shall be cut off,
But those who wait for the Lord shall not be cut short.
Yet a little while longer, and the wicked shall be no more
Though you'll look for them in their homes,
They will be gone.

But the meek shall inherit the land in the streets,
And delight themselves in it in abundance.
Prosperity rising out of poverty.

The wicked plot against the righteous,
Grind their teeth and ring great threats at them.
But the Lord laughs at the wicked,
Because He sees their day is coming to an end.

Be patient.
Wait for the Lord and keep to His ways
He will exalt you to inherit the land in your day.
You will see the destruction of the wicked
While the righteous remain pious,
Do good deeds, and pray.

69

Never envy a tyrant.

I have seen the wicked
Oppressing and vicious like dictators.
And after the Word addressed them,
They disappeared six days later.

Free the innocent,
And pay attention to the real rights.
For there is posterity and equality
For the peaceful's plights.

But the transgressors
Shall be destroyed altogether.
The prosperity of the wicked
Will be cut off and severed.

For the salvation of the righteous
Is from the Lord's divinity
For He is the refuge, yes indeed,
In the times when trouble is caused.
The Word helps and rescues them,
He saves them from the mayhem of the wicked
They take refuge in Him.

Amen.

"Before turning the page, take a few moments to reflect. Write down prayers, thoughts, or insights stirred in your heart. Let this page hold your conversation with God."

MacRoman 8:28 Threads of Grace

We already know, out at the deep end, how the threads get sewn. Every struggle, every victory, each one is a stitch in the grand design we're not shown. It's not just the smooth rides, not just the blessings and the shine; it's the storms and the scars, the bitter and the divine. When the heart breaks, and you feel that hollow sigh, when the tears turn to laughter, and you're lifted on a natural high. Your setbacks; That's the setup for the comeback, the redemption play, For the souls who walk with the Lord's hand, day after day. all things work together for good to those who love God and worship, those who have been called according to his purpose. He's the architect, the author, with the blueprint in His grasp. No moment's ever wasted, no memory meant to pass. He gathers the fragments, the long nights, the shattered days, and breathes His love through the chaos, weaving grace into the fray. We can't always trace the pattern, can't always see the threads, but He's composing every measure, where pain and purpose wed. That pain and ache you feel right now? It's the soil for your bloom. His promise never falters; His mercy never alters and makes you feel anew.

So, stand your ground, stay faithful—you belong to the dream, even in the shadows, you're part of His redeeming scheme. For the good of the prayers, for the ones who heed the call. He's always got you, and He won't let you fall.

"Before turning the page, take a few moments to reflect. Write down prayers, thoughts, or insights stirred in your heart. Let this page hold your conversation with God."

Believing Then Receiving

When Abraham and Sarah heard the Word
a promise from the Lord—it seemed absurd.
Too old, they thought, for such a gift,
their bodies were worn, their spirits adrift.

They ran ahead with frantic pace,
caught up in doubts, they lost their grace.
Instead of prayer, instead of trust,
they leaned on flesh, on schemes that bust.

Through Sarah's maid they sought to make
God's promise is real for their own sake.
But striving brought them only pain,
Hatred, tribulation, strife, and strain.

Yet Abraham learned, through patient years,
to trade his striving for his fears
that God's own promise needs no hand
to force it forth or make it stand.

You cannot push, what God will give,
or work your way to how to live.
The Kingdom doesn't bend or break
it opens to the eyes of your faith.

No manipulation, force, or plan,

no exhausting work of mortal man
just prayer and faith, and a humble heart,
and letting God perform His part.

Abraham believed, then he received,
fully persuaded, he successfully achieved
not by his doing, but by rest,
by trusting that God knows what is best.

At the right time—not soon, not late
God opened up that promised gate.
The blessings came, the gifts appeared,
when faith replaced what he had feared.

Believing then receiving, see?
That's how God's children come to be
the heirs of promises divine
not by our strength, but His design.

So lay your striving at His feet,
Let prayer and trust make you complete.
Be fully persuaded, stand and wait
God's timing is never late.
Amen.

Timeless Wisdom

One book can change your life, and the Bible has 66. God constantly shows His power through His messages. The New Testament runs concurrent with the Old, they interrelate. Even decades later, the Bible can be described in one word: Great. Only God is greater. The Bible may have translators to break barriers of languages, but the story still remains the same since Genesis. It stands still; it still stands to tell the story of God's glory and of the Son of Man. It's the most powerful message to mankind throughout the generations. It's life changing. God's wisdom and word are perfect from Genesis to Revelation. It's knowledgeable and fruitful. Its wisdom is rewarding. It's enriched food for thought. This book is rated the most important. Its wisdom is in this book for every situation and challenge you may be facing. You're guaranteed to be wiser if you obey it. It teaches how to live and conduct yourself on any assigned arrangements. This book never gets old or outdated, for it is timeless. It can also refute any critic and defend itself. It can hold its own weight on any scale. The word of God is imperishable. It's eternal. It's inspirational. It's sensational. It's non-partisan. It's authoritative, and it's influential. The almighty Holy Bible. The almighty Holy Bible. The one book that can change your life and be used for survival

"Before turning the page, take a few moments to reflect. Write down prayers, thoughts, or insights stirred in your heart. Let this page hold your conversation with God."

Make It Make Sense

God did not create you to live depressed,
Stressed out, worried, or oppressed.
He made you joyful, peaceful, content,
Full of love, patience, and heaven's intent.

Take an honest, elevated look at your life
Make it make sense — cut through the strife.
Is there joy deep down inside?
Do you wake up hopeful, or just in pride?

Are you enjoying your family and friends?
Or hiding away where the sadness never ends?
If not, what's stealing your joyrides?
Causing your peace to run and hide?
Come outside — don't live vexed,
Joy's not based on what happens next.
It's not in your status or success,
But in your will — that's the true test.

Will you stop stressing?
Will you start blessing?
"To rejoice in the Lord always" is a choice,
A decision, a lifted voice.

I know you're going to enjoy each day,

Whether things go right or drift astray.
Don't participate in hate — let love stay.
When everything goes wrong your way,
Pray… pray… pray.

Dig your heels in, hands to face,
Trust His timing, His perfect grace.
Go with the flow, don't lose control,
God's working all things for your soul.

Refuse to let those dark thoughts play,
Tune your mind to faith today.
Think joy, peace, hope, victory.
Believe that God holds your history.
He's in control — He'll make it well.
Choose joy, choose peace,
Choose to dwell…

With Him.
Amen.

Fruit-Bearing Tree

The Bible's word is the truth; I hold it here.
A breakthrough is coming through; I know it's near.
My God sees my struggles, the tribulation's fire,
Yet I cling to my faith; it's my soul's desire.
His words are my comfort in the darkest hour.
I won't let these cowards steal my joy or power.

The Almighty Lord is my fortress and my shield.
He embraced and refined me; my spirit was revealed.
I come to the Lord with all that remains,
I pray every night, trying to escape these chains.
Thank You, God, for the talents You placed deep in me.
Use me, send Your message, for all eyes to see.

My attitude is gratitude, praising Your Name,
Holy heaven's my goal, victory's my claim.
I'm a soldier of God, fulfilling my call,
I believe I can be the best of us all.
With God on my side, I shall not be distressed.
I walk through the shadows; my spirit is blessed.

The loyalty of God is brilliantly clear.
I'm prepared for the day when the Judge draws near.
I let the deep lessons of Jesus lead me on.

My spirit is renewed, like Ephesians' dawn.
No hiding, no silence, even when foes turned violent,
My poetry conquered poverty, loud and defiant.

I tithe because God is Love, King, and Supreme,
It's better to give than to greedily receive.
From false accusers, He set my soul free.
He gave wisdom, gave sight, and let my spirit just
breathe.
I planted my seeds in Jesus: a fruit-bearing tree.
Now I pray the youth will look and finally see.

Affirmation Psalm

I am good--like sunshine's warm embrace,
Warming the earth, filling every space.

I am great-- a tall tree reaching high,
Branches brushing dreams against the sky.

I am loved--a bird held safe in its nest,
Cradled by grace, in comfort and rest.

God loves me--a hand gentle and true,
Guiding my heart in everything I do.

My intentions are pure-- like waters so clear,
Flowing from springs that bring peace near.

I am beautiful-- I am handsome too,
Like wildflowers blooming with morning's dew.

Nothing can harm me-- a shield strong and bright,
Guarding my spirit through darkness and night.

I forgive myself-- letting stones roll away,
Freeing my soul for a brighter day.

I love myself-- a hug warm and tight,

Holding my heart through the coldest night.

No evil can prosper-- shadows fade in light,
Darkness retreats before what is right.

I will live in peace-- a stream calm and wide,
Flowing through me, with love as my guide.

I will love others-- and love myself too,
Sharing my heart in all that I do.

I will be kind--like soft rain from above,
Nourishing life with patience and love.

"I can do all things through him who strengthens me."
Philippians 4:13

Chapter 6: Realization and Revival

He Is Real

The Lord Jesus will return, like water to a desert.
He is my hope; the Lamb becomes the Shepherd.
He guides us to prolific pastures;
His word lead us down the straight and narrow path.
His parables give us advice.
He's the best counselor that you can ever have.

He is great, He is real;
He restored my life like
He did the tribes of Israel.
He is real!
I learned from His Testament,
which is instilled in my life's skills, still!

Through the blood of Christ, my sins are forgiven.
The only way to the Father is through the Son,
the One who has risen.
I strive to emulate His characteristics.
I strive to live a Christ-like life,
humbly and consistently.

I walk by faith In the dark valley of death;
He is my flashlight.
He is right when all the others left.
My mistakes I learn from with hindsight.

I love the Lord's discipline; it keeps my mind right.

I strive to live a Christ-like life,
and you are too!
If you're here, I suppose.
If you believe that Christ died for our sins
and on the third day He rose,
He conquered death and the insults of His foes.

They didn't kill Him; He's majesty.
He chose to live out His prophecy through blasphemy.
Now He sits on the right hand of the Throne.
He lived a perfect life to show us actually
flawless behavior, to strive through our tragedies.

And when He returns, every tongue will confess,
Every heart renewed, every soul blessed.
The Lamb who was slain forever will reign,
The Shepherd of grace who conquered our pain.

Prodigal Son

"While he was still a long way off. his father saw him and was filled with compassion for him; he ran to his son, threw his arms around him and kissed him."
Luke 15:20

The father in this parable represents our God,
His heart of compassion, forgiving and broad.
When we've sinned and wandered off course,
He runs to embrace us, His love is His force.

Notice in Scripture, the prodigal's return,
The father came running, no trace of concern.
It's God in the spirit, sprinting in love,
Toward a young thug, unworthy thereof.

Filthy with mud, with hogs he had lain,
Yet mercy rushed out to erase all the shame.
The same son who left, who disgraced his name,
Involved in wickedness, drowning in blame.

That same son—like many today,
Drinking, drugging, lost in the fray.
Hustling hard, sinning, embarrassing his soul,
Living life empty, without self-control.

God could've run to heal the lame,
To teach, to preach, to earn acclaim.
But instead, He ran to one who'd failed,
Whose brokenness told how sin had prevailed.

Someone sick and tired, worn and weak,
Whose worth the world refused to speak.
Yet God still ran because He can relate,
With arms wide open, full of grace innate.

The enemy works overtime with lies,
Convincing hearts that God not alive
He wants mistrust, confusion, doubt,
to make us feel we're counted out.

But what if we believed His love is true,
That God forever runs toward you?
How much freer, more secure we'd live,
Knowing He's ready for our sins to forgive.

Even when we fall, when we lose our way,
He waits with compassion every day.
Don't wait, don't let lies seal your fate
Escape Satan's mental rape, before it's too late.

Rearranged

Yeah, I'm back again, but still standing on the Rock.
Through the struggle and the pain, my praying will never
stop.
The enemy's been plotting, trying to knock me off my feet,
But I got the spirit of Jonah, so I'm moving through the beast.

They don't understand the armor that I'm strapped in daily
Sword of the Spirit cutting through, ain't nothing gonna
phase me.
I was lost in the darkness, caught up in the world's schemes,
But Christ pulled me out the mud now I'm living out His
dreams.

I ain't perfect — I stumble and I fall,
But His grace picks me up every time I make that call.
They see me moving different, wonder why I changed,
Because the old me died with Christ—I've been rearranged.

From the cell block to the Cross, that's my testimony.
He turned my mess into a message — now the devil fears
me.
I'm repping for the Kingdom while I'm walking through the
fire;
The devil is a liar — my faith's higher than the trials he
conspires.

So, when you see me, know I'm covered by His blood

90

Not by my own strength, but by the Father's love.
I'm a soldier in this battle, holding down my post,
Living for the Father, Son, and the Holy Ghost.

Amen

"Before turning the page, take a few moments to reflect. Write down prayers, thoughts, or insights stirred in your heart. Let this page hold your conversation with God."

Idolatry: The Hidden Danger

Idolatry isn't just bulls or calves you see,
It's chains, its phones,
the things you cling to secretly.
It's whatever comes to mind
when you think of God above,
If it isn't Holy God Almighty, then it's a dub.

Get your values in order, get your priorities tight,
Idolatry can blind you, keep you from the Light.
You better pray. His ways are not like ours,
His thoughts are infinite, higher than the stars.

There's enough revelation to show there's more,
Beyond the sun, moon, and stars that we adore.
Idols are counterfeit, they'll never amount to Christ,
No matter their price—they're empty, iced.

Idolatry is attachments,
Devotions gone wrong,
To something other than God,
Where the heart doesn't belong.

Modern-day Baals
Chains, pendants, jewelry, and images,
Things that steal your heart,
Fill your mind with scrimmages.

Isaiah 44:9—listen close, take heed:
"Whoever makes an idol is not improved or freed."
So, kill your impulses, loose sex, and impure actions,
Wicked thoughts, greed, unchecked lust, and
distractions.

Avoid them at all costs. Don't give them a place,
Idle idols vanish; they're nothing to embrace.
God is the God of all gods, jealous, fierce, and true,
His rivals are nothing—He will pierce them through.

So, turn your heart fully, let God take His throne,
Let nothing, not nothing, claim the love He alone owns.

Exodus 20:3, "You shall have no other gods before me

False Gods

Let me break it down real clear,
Idolatry ain't just statues, it's whatever you hold dear.
More than God Almighty, more than the Most High,
Could be your money, your status, or the image you
glorify.

Check your heart, what are you chasing every day?
Is it likes and views, or walking in His way?
Because idols creep subtle,
they don't announce their name,
Could be your career, your girl, your ride, your fame.

We put God in a box, try to make Him fit our minds,
Create a version that's comfortable, gentle, and kind.
But the God of Abraham doesn't bow to what we think,
He's holy fire, not some custom-made link.

Modern-day Baal wrapped in designer clothes,
Golden chains around our necks, but shackles on our
souls.
We worship at the altar of the gram and the Tube,
Sacrificing real connection for the digital mood.

Isaiah said it plain: these idols had no worth,
Can't save, can't speak, just dust upon the earth.

But we stay devoted to the temporary high,
Chasing satisfaction that'll never satisfy.

Check those earthly impulses that be leading you astray,
Lust, greed, and pride keep you from the way.
Guard your thoughts, check your heart,
examine what you praise,
Because the God of gods is jealous,
His attention shall be paid.

He doesn't play about His glory,
doesn't compete for second place,
Either He's your everything
or you're running in the wrong race.
So break them chains, smash them idols,
make your choice today
Bow before the King of Kings, let Him lead the way.

Matthew 6:24
24 "No one can serve two masters. Either you will hate the one and love the other, or you will be devoted to the one and despise the other. You cannot serve both God and money.

Chapter 7: Lament and Deliverance

Macpsalm 54: Save Me, O God

Save me, O God, by Your holy name
Vindicate me with Your strength and flame.
Judge me.
by my faith and Your strength throughout
Hear my prayers, Lord;
Give ear to the words of my mouth.

For strangers and enemies rise against me.
oppressors who seek my freedom and my soul.
for they have not placed You before themselves.
They will not let go.
I need Your help!
Behold, my God is my helper.
The Lord Christ stands against those
Who strives to uphold my soul.
He shall repay my enemies with their own evilness.
and cut them off from Your truth in astonishment.

I will freely sacrifice my mind.
my body and my soul unto You, as I should.
I will praise Your holy name, Lord.
for it is greatly good.

For You have delivered me out of all my troubles,
and I have seen You defeat all my enemies.
That is why I love You.

Amen.

"Before turning the page, take a few moments to reflect. Write down prayers, thoughts, or insights stirred in your heart. Let this page hold your conversation with God."

A Fragile Raft

The world's a blur, a washed-out grey,
My eyes are pools that hold the day,
But all I see is grief and pain,
A drowning heart, a soul in the rain.
I'm blinded by the tears, as I weep,
Lost in the shadows, buried deep.

I'm dying inside, a slow decay,
Each sunrise bleeds to yesterday.
A silent scream, a hidden plea,
Can someone, anyone, help me please?
This crushing weight, this hollow ache,
My spirit's breaking, for goodness's sake.

The devils dance, a swirling throng,
They sing their lies, where I went wrong.
Recycling my soul, piece by piece,
Distracting and robbing me of inner peace.

Evil spirits whisper low,
Trying to mold me, so I can fold
Into a creature dark and grim,
Lost from the light, hope, and hymn.
In the sea of this life, I barely stay,
A fragile raft that drifts away.
The waves crash high, the currents pull,

My weakened strength begins to dull.
Through troubled times, I clutch God so tight,
Until I can see a distant glimmer of the light.
I seek for hope, a guiding star,
To lead me back, from where I are.

I know I can swim, I feel the urge,
But this ocean's depths relentlessly purge
The strength I have, the will to fight,
These waters deep, steal might.
My chances thin, a string-bean string,
But ain't no quit in me—psalms I'll sing.
A song of struggle, raw and true,
A testament to making moves to break through.

Right now, I'm lost, I cannot find
A path of solace for my mind.
Played with fire, felt the searing flame,
And now I'm consumed by this game.

So, hear my pleas, a whispered prayer,
To break these chains and banish despair.
Unblind my eyes, dry up these tears,
And calm the raging, inner fears.
Help me to rise, to stand anew,
And find the strength to see it through.
To reclaim my soul, to find my worth,
And walk free again, upon this Earth.

Echoes of the Soul

Blinded by tears, a world unseen,
A heavy curtain, dark and mean.
Inside you wither, then slowly fade,
A silent scream, a soul betrayed.

Devils gather, a circling pack,
To tear me apart, to steal me back.
Recycle my soul, a twisted game,
Whispering horrors, fueled by flame.

Evil spirits, with lying breaths,
Trying to drown me into death.
Confide in the mold, they softly say.
But I'll fight their grip and break away.
In life's commotion ocean, I barely stay,
Afloat on the surface, day by day.

.

Troubled waters, a churning sea,
Yet it's hope I seek, desperately.
I know I can swim; God's strength resides.
But depths are vast, where darkness hides.
Chances are slim; the odds are steep.
But soft, I am not; His promise he keeps.
The mirror reflects a stranger's face.
A haunted gaze, in time and space.

"Look," it whispers, "what life has done."
A shattered spirit, victory undone

Now in my forties, stressed and worn,
Unworthy feelings, my life is torn.

Depressed and lost, life's messy scene,
I played with fire and felt the burning gleam.
But listen close to the words unheard,
Beneath the pain, under the verge

A flicker of strength, a resilient seed,
A burning ember, a vital need.
To rise above, to break the chains,
To wash away the years of pain.

To fight the demons, face the fear,
And know that, my help is near.
Seek out the light, and sing a psalm,
A hand to hold, a helping palm.

Let kindness guide, and love restore,
The shattered pieces, to ask for more.
I am not broken, just deeply scarred,
A warrior's heart, forever hard.

So, I'll wipe my tears, and clear my sight,
Embrace the dawn and claim my light.
Find my footing, strong and true,
A worthy soul, forever rule

Let hope to ignite, a yearning desire
And rise above the burning fires.

Dark Valleys

As I step in the shadows in the Valley of Death, holding my breath, while holding on to regrets. I wish I would've left much sooner than I did. Now I'm in the county with a bounty, clueless as to what I did. When I was arraigned in court, I was entertained by the thought of maybe this is just a movie or a mistake until my name got called. Now I'm in this cell, restrained and forced. This is similar to hell, but I have to maintain it, of course.

God, do You hear me? Are You listening? I'm clearly sorry for once again being in this position. I can't blame anybody but myself for this predicament, making acquisitions with promiscuous women. Sex was my intention. Lord, please forgive me for committing adultery. Please console me, consult me, for I am weak in the flesh. Please help me. They're making false accusations, naming me. It's ironic how they only chastise Black men for white slavery. Now they're shipping me. I don't know where this Black SUV is taking me, across state lines to Philly FDC, maybe. They're trying to claim that I affected interstate commerce, but there was no money in her purse.

I should've put God first, but I somehow got distracted by all the worldly attractions. It happens... I gave in to Satan. To Lucifer's satisfaction, he wants me in the trunk of a police car or a hearse, and my life redacted from the Book of Life. Consequences of my actions. I was weak to the lures, the evil diversions that came my way, but I know You have a deeper purpose for me. I pray,

I seek forgiveness. Lord, let me find Your grace. God Almighty, when I bear witness for Your sake, please deliver me from the systemic racial evils. Don't let these people use me and unjustly cause me harm. The courts are unequal. Please, Lord, redeem me from my enemies who seek to devour my last energy, trying to put an end to me. Let the wicked false accusers be put to blame. Clear my name of any wrongdoings so I can clarify my fame. Let Your face shine on me in your son's name.

I claim. I'm forgiven for my sins because for us he had to hang. He has hung on the cross. His loss was our gain, but He rose and chose to be love for us, not just the ones who actually believe. So please forgive me, even though I'm far from perfect, but I do love others, pay tithes to churches, and worship. You're my God. My time is in Your hands and in mercy. not the judgment of that of a man or woman.

Everything that happens is in Your plans. I trust my life with You, even though I may not understand. I walk blind to you. in the shadows with You as my GPS, even when the courtroom goons want to see me less. I know this can't be my fate. won't concede to the stress. It won't end here in jail. Inshallah, I will prevail. I will be with my Lord. I can't fail. I dwell in the House of Integrity and profess I'm protected all day and night for life. I've been tested.

Sealed in the Spirit: A Mother's Prayer

Heavenly Father,
I lift up my mom to You. Please bring her comfort and
healing. Your Word says: "He heals the brokenhearted
and binds up their wounds" Let her in the Holy spirit be
sealed in. Lord, touch her body and spirit, and give her
peace. I trust Your promise that "the prayer of faith will
save the one who is sick, and the Lord will raise him up" I
will pray for her and not cease. Strengthen her and
surround her with Your love. In Jesus' name, Amen.

"Before turning the page, take a few moments to reflect. Write down prayers, thoughts, or insights stirred in your heart. Let this page hold your conversation with God."

From Gleaning to Glory

A young widow in the morning light,
Dreams turned to dust, her hope out of sight.
Yet Ruth rose up with steadfast grace,
Made God her refuge, found her place.

She could have nursed her bitter loss,
Could have refused to bear the cross
Of caring for another's need,
But love became her faithful creed.

Dawn after dawn, she walked the fields,
Gathering what the harvest yields—
The scattered grain, the leftovers,
A life of lack stretched over.

But Heaven sees what earth forgets:
The faithful heart that never quits,
The one who serves through tears and pain,
The one who trusts the sun will shine again.

You are not trapped by tragedy,
You are not bound by what you didn't see,
Not limited by absent voices,
By broken dreams or stolen choices.

God holds the universe in His hands;

He architects what you can't plan.
One day, a wealthy man saw her there—
Boaz beheld her beauty fair.

From gleaning scraps at break of day,
To owning fields where workers pray,
From a widow's grief to honor's throne,
From borrowed grain to all she'd own.

This is the promise waiting still:
Keep climbing up that faithful hill.
Put God first in the morning hour;
He's orchestrating His divine power.

The right eyes will observe your worth,
Your steps are ordered here on earth.
New doors will swing on sudden hinges;
Promotion comes on golden fringes.

Don't believe the lying voice
That says you have no other choice.
Keep being faithful, kind, and true,
And watch what God will do through you.

From the field to the estate,
From barely enough to abundance great,
The gleaner becomes the honored bride—
That's what happens when in God you abide.

When Trials Become Thresholds

In the shadow of a cruel man's pride,
Where rage rode swift and justice died,
One woman stood with wisdom's grace
Abigail, who changed fate's face.

Between the sword and senseless death,
She spoke with measured, holy breath,
"This fool is not worth vengeance's stain,
Your destiny holds greater gain."

How many lives turn on such choices?
How many souls find stronger voices
When circumstances press them down,
Yet still they rise and claim their crown?

We carry reasons, worn and true,
For living bitter, broken through
The wounds of childhood, love's betrayal,
The door that closed, the plans that failed.

But every excuse becomes a chain
That binds us to our grief and pain,
While those who honor what is right
Transform their darkness into light.

This is the test that shapes your story:
Will you trade purpose for your worry?
Will you let unfairness write your name,
Or rise above and stake your claim?

Stand firm when life seems set to break you,
Know that trials come to make you
What appears to stop your sacred way
Is setting up your finest day.

For in the furnace, gold is proven,
And stagnant waters, once they're moving,
Become the rivers, deep and wide,
Where greatness learns to turn the tide.

Be Abigail amid your sorrow,
Honor God and face your tomorrows
Your integrity will pave the road
To blessings you have not yet known.

Help Me Please (Psalm of Pain)

Help me please, God.
Send your angels to snatch me from pain.
I'm living life in vain.
It feels like there's ice in my veins.
I'm cold at night when it rains.
It hides my tears. Confined to a tier
for, like, five of my years.
Why am I here?
I didn't commit this crime.
That chick is lying.
It was my chips she was eyeing.
Because of my skin,
I'm automatically guilty.
Free me? Still don't see any wins.
This system is filthy.
The enemy is trying to kill me.
Bury me inside.
My family doesn't feel me.
Think I'm barely alive.
I don't really want to die.
I just need a change of scenery.
I don't know why.
This life can't really be that mean to me.
If it is—then take me right now.
How can I live in a world so foul?
The only thing I can do now,
is to get down On my knees,
Pray to God for forgiveness...
Can you help me, please?

"Before turning the page, take a few moments to reflect. Write down prayers, thoughts, or insights stirred in your heart. Let this page hold your conversation with God."

Chapter 8: Praise and Gratitude

Macpsalm 66: *The Sound of His Praise*

Shout! Shout! Shout joyfully to the Lord!
May the whole earth sing of the honor, glory,
and the magnificence of His name.
Make His praise glorious!
Say to God, "How awesome are Your works!
Because of the greatness of Your power,
even Your enemies will pretend to obey You
as they try to hide their dirt"
All the earth will bow down to worship You,
singing praises to Your holiness's sake.
and to the loving-kindness of Your ways.
Come and see the works of God
He is awesome in His deeds
toward the children of men.
He turned the sea into dry land;
His people crossed through the river as planned.
They rejoiced in Him and in the strength
of His mighty hand.
The Almighty God rules by His powerful might.
His eyes keep watch over the world;
do not let the rebellious rise up in pride.
Those who worship their possessions
and cling to treasures that rust and fade
their wealth will not last forever.
For even them God has made.
Bless our God, my people!
Let the sound of His praise
be heard around the world!

He keeps us among the living,
delivers us from trouble,
and does not allow our feet to stumble.
For You have tested us, O God;
You have refined us as silver is refined.
You brought us into the net,
laid heavy burdens upon our minds,
You have allowed men to rule over us in defeat.
We went through fire and through water
and still, we stood on our feet.
Yet You brought us out into a place of abundance.
I will come into Your house with tithes and offerings;
I will pay the vows my mouth spoke
when I was in distress and broke.
Yes, I will offer to You not only wealth,
but works of service and gratitude.
Come and hear, all who love and fear God,
and I will testify to what He has done for me.
I cried aloud to Him;
He was praised upon my tongue in loyalty.
If I had cherished sin in my heart,
the Lord would not have heard me
He has attended to the voice of my prayer.
but surely God has heard me;
Blessed be the Lord,
who has not turned away my prayers,
nor withheld His love and kindness from me.
He always showed me He cared. Amen

Apples that are good

I don't want to wake up grumpy,
I usually just let her sleep.
I have a gratitude attitude,
praising my Father who's heavenly,
for the holy heaven is my destiny.
I am a soldier of the Lord, like I was destined to be.
I believe that I can be the best that I can be.
With God on my side, I shall not fret nor weep,
no weapons can prosper or affect me deep.
I will stay awake tho I will not sleep

For I shall walk in the valley, in the shadows, with tears.
God's loyalty for me is not always clear.
I will not be scared, just prepared for D Day.
I will let the lessons of Jesus lead thee way.

I renewed my spirit like Chapter 4 of Ephesians,
changed my ways like the apostles Paul and Peter did.
I neither hid nor have I gone silent,
even when the oppressors got shady and violent.
I used my talents to rise above poverty.
I pay my tithes because God is Love and Sovereignty.

He's King. It's better to give than to receive.
He never leaves me alone,

He always gives me what I need,
That's why I still believe.

I was facing the law with false accusers.
He set me free. He let me breathe through the sewer.
I prayed with wisdom and understanding.
God came through like He always planned it.
He let me see. I planted my seeds;
it grew into a fruit-bearing tree.
I hope through me the youth can see,
a work that's in progress so they can achieve.

Ephesians 4:22-24

*22 You were taught, with regard to your former way of life,
to put off your old self, which is being corrupted by its deceitful desires; 23 to be
made new in the attitude of your minds; 24 and to put on the new self, created
to be like God in true righteousness and holiness.*

I'm Grateful Too

I'm grateful
for clean air to breathe,
I'm grateful
for serene mind and soul at ease,
I'm grateful
for God's mercy, giving me chance to be great,
I'm grateful
for waking well, with words that elate.
I'm grateful
for warm water to wash away dirt on my palm,
I'm grateful
for peaceful streets, where I walk with no harm,
I'm grateful
for freedom that banishes fear of the beast,
I'm grateful
for the Lord, saving me—from me, released.
I'm grateful
for a platform where my poetry can fly,
I'm grateful
to speak truth, unbound, to build or destroy a lie,
I'm grateful
as poetic pirate, I chart ships of fellowship and throne,
I'm grateful
to be fully alive—not walking dead, but wholly grown.

"Before turning the page, take a few moments to reflect. Write down prayers, thoughts, or insights stirred in your heart. Let this page hold your conversation with God."

Psalm of Fearless Faith
(Inspired by Psalm 27)

Jesus is my light and my salvation—
whom shall I fear in this broken nation?
Jesus is the rock of my soul and my life,
of whom shall I be afraid, through trouble or strife?

When wicked opps rise up with hate,
it's my enemies and foes who stumble at the gate.
Though an army swarms from every place,
my heart stands firm—I won't fear their face.

Though war breaks out and chaos reigns,
I'm confident in Him, through losses and gains.
Never complacent, I trust His direction
my refuge, my fortress, my divine protection.

One thing I ask, one thing I seek:
His grace, His presence, His voice when He speaks.
To dwell in the house of the Lord all my days,
to bask in His beauty, to walk in His ways.

In trouble's hour, He keeps me safe,
in His sacred tent, I find my place.
He lifts me high—above inflation, above the noise,
above temptation, above the ploys.

Then my head is exalted, lifted above,
surrounded by enemies, still crowned in His love.
At His tent I'll shout with joy, unashamed
I'll sing, I'll praise, I'll lift His name.

Hear my voice when I call, O Jesus
be merciful, answer, and never leave us.
Your love is my anthem, my shelter, my song;
with You by my side, I know I belong.

Psalm 27:1: "The Lord is my light and my salvation; whom shall I fear? The Lord is the stronghold of my life; of whom shall I be afraid?"

Dear God Dear Lord

Dear God, Dear Lord, I hope you hear me
I hope you protect me,
I hope you are watching over me
I hope you show me favor
I'm taking care of myself and my neighbor
I am helping others out; I am protecting the weak
I pray night and day, even before I go to sleep
I read my scriptures and pray all day
I'm doing the best that I can in this mind state
Please watch over me and love me
Dear Lord, protect me and watch over my family

In this concrete cage where time moves slow
I bow my head and let my spirit let God let go
To You, the Most Merciful, the Most High
The One who hears when broken men cry

I know I've stumbled, I know I've fallen short
But I come before You in this humble court
Not with excuses, not with empty pleas
But with a willing heart, bent on my knees
You see me here when no one else can see
The man I'm building, who I'm trying to be

Beyond these walls, this number and this cell
You know my story, only You can tell
I wake before the sun begins to rise
To speak Your name beneath these grey prison skies

I ask for strength to face another day

I ask for wisdom and discernment to know what to say
When younger brothers come to me confused
When they've been broken down and been abused
By this system, by their past, by their own pain
I try to be the shelter in their rain

I share my commissary when I see someone in need
I break up fights before they make somebody bleed
I teach the alphabet to those who never learned to read
I plant Your word's Holy tree like it's a sacred seed

Because You said to love our neighbor as ourselves
And in this place, we're all on the same shelves
We're all just broken vessels seeking light
Trying to make it right through another night

So I read Your words in both the tongues You've spoken
The Bible's promise, the Moses's golden token
I find You in the verses, in the stories of the prophets
Who faced their trials and never tried to stop it

Moses in the wilderness, Joseph in the pit
Jesus in the garden, David in the midst
Between the old life and the new calling
They all kept standing even when they were falling

And so I stand, dear God, dear Lord, I stand
With Your holy books trembling in my hand
With every page I turn, I feel You near
With every verse I memorize, I conquer fear

Please watch over my mother while I'm gone

Give her strength to keep holding on
Let her know that all her prayers aren't in vain
That her son is changing, growing through the pain

Watch over my brother, give him peace of mind
Help him forgive the trouble I've caused,
help him be kind
To himself, for any guilt he bears
Remind him that You answer all his prayers

Protect my sisters, keep their spirit bright
Don't let my absence steal her light
Watch over my niece, watch my nephews grow
Guide them in the ways they need to know
Keep them far from paths that led me here
Shield them from the violence, from the fear
Let them learn from my mistakes without the pain
Let sunshine follow them, not this rain

And God, if it's Your will, show me favor in this place
Let the judge see something worthy in my face
Let mercy tip the scales when my time comes
Let me walk back to my family, back to my loved ones
But even if that's not Your plan for me
Even if these walls are where I'm meant to be
I'll accept it as Your wisdom, not Your curse
I'll use this time to make myself immerse
In Your teachings, in Your love, in Your ways
I'll be a light in darkness every single day
I'll help the weak, protect those who can't defend
I'll be the brother, teacher, helper, and the friend
Because You put me here for a reason I can't see

Maybe I'm supposed to save somebody else, not me
Maybe my purpose in this season of my life
Is to be a testament through struggle and through strife

So I surrender to Your will, I bow my head
I thank You for my life, for my daily bread
I thank You for another breath, another chance
To grow closer to You in this circumstance
Guide my steps when I don't know the way
Give me patience when I want to stray
Give me courage when I feel afraid
Give me faith that never will fade

Forgive my sins, wash them clean
Help me become what I've never been
A righteous man, a faithful son
A servant devoted until my work is done

And when my time on Earth is through
Let me stand worthy before You
Not perfect, but transformed by grace
Ready to see You face to face
Until that day, I'll keep my head bowed low
I'll keep my heart open to Your flow
I'll be the man You always knew I could be
I'll honor You in captivity and when I'm free

Ameen. Amen. So be it, Lord.
I trust in Your mercy, I trust in Your word.
In Jesus' name and God's light,
I pray this prayer both day and night.

Chapter 9: Salvation and Service

Alive

We have deliverance in Christ.
He spiritually guides us through
With the Holy Spirit, parables, and advice.
He gives us energy from His ministry,
According to Chapter 4, Verse 1, in 1 Timothy.
But some will abandon the faith freely
And follow deceivers willingly
Only my God, in humility,
Will I praise, for He is awesome.
He makes my allotment secure,
For He is my cup and my portion.
He saves people from the wilderness
And the Devil's bewilderment.
My hope is in God's strength
And wisdom; I'm obedient.
When it comes to my Father,
I am never lacking.
As it happens, faith works better with action.
When I am weak, it is the Lord whom I call,
And when He disciplines me, I shall take heed,
Lest I fall.
I shall activate faith
Through trials and tribulations.
I shall lean on the Lord,
For He is mightier than any sword or nation.
He is the King of all kings;
He isn't dead, He's alive.
He is holy and dignified.
He is our Lord and Savior, Jesus Christ.

"Before turning the page, take a few moments to reflect. Write down prayers, thoughts, or insights stirred in your heart. Let this page hold your conversation with God."

Healer

The Lord is near to you.
your healer, your strength.
He whispers: "I am the Lord who heals you."
Do not be afraid; you are kept.
for He holds you close in His arms.
He will give you rest.
and His peace will guard your heart,
steady and unshakable.
Lean on Him, trust in His ways,
for He is faithful,
and His love will not let you go astray.

Isaiah 41:10
*"Do not fear, for I am with you; do not be dismayed, for I am your God. I will
strengthen you and help you; I will uphold you with my righteous right hand."*

"Before turning the page, take a few moments to reflect. Write down prayers, thoughts, or insights stirred in your heart. Let this page hold your conversation with God."

Unique

God made me in His image.
I am His creation.
I am I of I, with my own DNA.
I have a soul, a uniqueness

I am important to my Father God,
The One who miraculously crafted me
In my mother's womb.
To Him, I am extraordinary and very special too.
I am His fruit
from His Tree of Life that has been pruned,

I have been refined, and made to flourish.
I'm loved by God, in my heart He is stored in.
Psalm 138:2:
"I will praise You with all my heart for Your unfailing
love."
Even when I don't love myself,
MY GOD is faithful,
MY GOD is there to help.
To Him—and only Him—I give praise.
To nobody else.

"Before turning the page, take a few moments to reflect. Write down prayers, thoughts, or insights stirred in your heart. Let this page hold your conversation with God."

Come Save me

Only by your grace, your mercy, will I be led to safety. I'm being persecuted by people that hate me. I don't know why. Maybe it's because they hate men, or maybe it's because of my skin or my kin, which is Christ. Through his blood, I was saved, but temptations and sensations have me running away to the roads that Satan has paved. But I walk by faith, so I'm able to face Satan and tribulations with confidence. Throughout the day, I pray, praise, and repent, asking the Lord for forgiveness. I know he will come save me, for he is my hope and my strength. I even pray for my enemies because God deals with my vengeance. I'm depending on the Lord to come save me. All of my eggs are in his basket; I'm all in. I know he will keep me from falling. Through my faith, I activated his grace. Now I'm calling on the Lord to come save me.

Only by your grace and your mercy will I be led to safety. I'm being persecuted by people that hate me. I don't know why. Maybe it's because I am wise, or that I am intelligent, or that I'm independent. Or is it that I no longer need the government's assistance, nor am I still indigent? I use the Lord as my strength and the knowledge of his word, especially in Proverbs, to help me rise up out of poverty. Love is a verb which is given to me constantly through his Holy Sovereignty. This holy Trinity Deity is what guides me, and that sweet "pie in the sky" as a prize resounds in me.

My hope is in you, Lord. Come save me. Only by your grace and your mercy will I be led to safety. I'm being persecuted by people that hate me. I don't know why. Is it because I'm handsome and made in God's image? But I'm not boastful, just hopeful, humble, and a faithful Christian that isn't afraid or timid. The Lord favors me. My enemies plot with negative energy, trying to put an end to me so brazenly. But my God is the God of all gods; he is almighty. He will make a way out of no way, yes indeed, so why try me? They slyly slander me. They hate on me viciously and consistently. But my faith is in the Lord. He is my shield, my retreat. My hope is in the Lord.

Come save me. Only by your grace, your mercy, will I be led to safety. I'm being persecuted by people that hate me. I don't know why. Lord, here save me.

Psalm 142:5–7 (NIV)"I cry to you, Lord; I say, "You are my refuge, my portion in the land of the living." Listen to my cry, for I am in desperate need; rescue me from those who pursue me, for they are too strong for me. Set me free from my prison, that I may praise your name"

God's Got You

God's got you, no matter what you've been through,
Don't stress your future. He's already working for you.
Through struggles and pain, His love will shine through,
God's got you, He's faithful, His Word is true.

He answers your prayers, accepts who you are,
With His strength and His grace, you're gonna go far.
You're a star in His galaxy, shining so bright,
He's the sun in your sky, lighting up the night.
God's got you.

In your darkest hour, He's your power, your fire,
He lifts your spirit, raises you higher.
God's got you, every valley, every hill,
When life knocks you down, He's the hand that is still.

He gave us His Son, so all we must do is believe,
God's got the rest, your heart will receive.
He blesses your life, better than Aleve can heal,
God's got you, every sickness, every trial, every ordeal.

His Word holds the answers to a life that's blessed,
No need to second-guess. He knows what's best.
He's the way when there's no way, the light in your
doubt,
God's got you, trust Him, He'll work it out.

Got questions? He's got answers,
no need for false guides,
Ignore the gossip, the lies, the worldly tides.
No fake friends, no frienemies, no devil's disguise,
God's got you, His truth will open your eyes.

Praise Him when you wake, praise Him at night,
Pray when it's stormy, pray when it's tight.
God's got you, He's holding you through,
He's faithful, He's true, He's making all things new.

Jeremiah 29:11
11 For I know the plans I have for you," declares the Lord, "plans to prosper you and not to harm you, plans to give you hope and a future.

Through Fire and Faith

I cried out in the silence with my heart full of despair,
"Why, Lord, why me? Is anyone there?"
The storm raged around me, the night never ceased,
My soul felt abandoned, my spirit had no peace.

I watched my dreams crumble, my world falls apart,
Pain carved its mark deep into my broken heart.
Friends spoke in riddles, whispers full of blame,
I searched for Your face yet only felt my shame.

I questioned Your justice, I doubted Your plan,
I felt small and forsaken, a weak, trembling man.
The weight of my suffering pressed down like stone,
I wondered if my injustices would ever be fully known.

But still, in the shadows, I clung to a thread,
A whisper inside me: "Keep trusting instead."
Though my voice shook, I spoke to the sky,
Even in anger, I refused to get high or die.

Days turned to nights, and nights turned to days,
Patience was my armor; faith was my only praise.
The fire refined me, the trial was my test,
I learned that Your timing always best.

Then the clouds parted, light broke through the rain,
Joy returned softly, washing away the pain.
Blessings poured over, more than I could measure,
Riches of spirit, and grace without treasure.

The house I had lost, the harvest destroyed,
will be restored double, as Your hand deployed.
Family and friends returned to my side,
Peace settled deep where sorrow once cried.

I learned that doubt is human, yet patience is divine,
Those trials may bend us but never confine.
Blessing comes slowly, reward after strife,
Faith held in the dark yields a triumphant life.

Job 23:10
But he knows the way that I take;
when he has tested me, I will come forth as gold.

Seek Your Face

My heart whispers in the quiet:
"Seek His face."
And I answer, trembling yet sure.
Your face, O Lord, I will seek.
Hide not from me, my Helper,
For I am your son that remembers Your breath.
Do not turn away in anger.
For You have carried me when I fell.
If father and mother forget my name,
Still, You will gather me close.
Your arms are my inheritance;
Your mercy is my home.
Teach me Your ways, O Lord;
lead me straight through the noise of enemies,
through the false words and shadowed looks.
You are my compass in confusion,
my calm in the crowd's accusations.
I am confident of this:
I will see Your greatness
not only beyond the grave,
but here, in wastefulness
in the land of the living dead
I still hold Your sacredness.
So I will wait.
strong in surrender,
steadied by grace,
and take heart in the silence,
For all my sins are forgiven.

"Before turning the page, take a few moments to reflect. Write down prayers, thoughts, or insights stirred in your heart. Let this page hold your conversation with God."

Embrace praise

God, Father, thank You that You are my Almighty God who runs to meet me even when I've made mistakes, and when times are hard. When things aren't so great and I have gotten off course, thank You that Your arms are always held wide open and welcoming, and that Your love always restores me. Thank You, Lord, for being for me, even when my friends and family ignore me. I thank You for being with me in the lion's den when sent me there by my lying friends. You protected me when I was being oppressed and the authorities disrespected me. You never neglected me and accepted me when I came back to the path. All my friends laughed, but You took me in Your grasp. I declare that I am going to walk in peace and be confident that You are for me.

Amen.

"Before turning the page, take a few moments to reflect. Write down prayers, thoughts, or insights stirred in your heart. Let this page hold your conversation with God."

About Author

Coolgmack is a voice forged in the concrete jungles of Westchester and NYC, a poet who turned pain into purpose. After graduating from Sleepy Hollow High, his path led him through Rikers Island, an experience that sharpened his words into weapons of truth.

Though he is still serving an unjust, perpetual sentence from a crime committed 20 years ago that carried only a 10-year term, Coolgmack does not let that deter him. From behind bars, he channels the grit of survival and the ache of injustice into his work. Poetry remains his sanctuary, his megaphone, and his redemption, fueling his fight against injustices in Amerikkka. Coolgmack is an author, publisher, and entrepreneur on a mission to spark a revolution through revelation, helping communities uncover their inner strength. His latest work, including "poetic injustices in Amerikkka," is a testament to the holy fusion of pain, passion, and purpose.

Find him everywhere the ink spills—on all social media platforms, including TikTok, YouTube, Twitter, and Instagram, where he is universally known as @coolgmack, or visit his website at coolgmack.com.

More books by Coolgmack

Find all these titles on amazon.com
coolgmack.com   etc.

"POETIC INJUSTICE$ IN AMERIKKKA" by Coolgmack is a powerful lyrical analysis of systemic racism in America. This thought-provoking work provides firsthand insight into institutional racism while advocating for economic and social restitution for Black Americans. examines historical oppression and its impact on current socioeconomic structures, race relations, and politics. He argues for changing the rules of economic opportunity so everyone has a fair chance to succeed. Drawing from multigenerational community experiences, he passes down ancestral wisdom and survival strategies, reminding his people they are enough and encouraging them to choose life beyond pain and trauma.

offers a raw and unfiltered look at the complexities of love. In this powerful collection, he navigates the tumultuous journey from **heartbreak and betrayal** to the unwavering pursuit of a love that is true and lasting. *Sucker4Love* is a testament to the pain and triumph of human connection. With a voice that is both vulnerable and resilient, Coolgmack exposes the deep scars of past relationships while holding onto the hope for a future defined by genuine intimacy and devotion.

This is a book for anyone who has ever been a **"sucker for love"**—who has given their all and lost, only to rise again with a stronger belief in the power of an honest heart

Sucker4love Too: "Love Ain't Logical its lyrical" is a soul-baring collection of poetry from coolgmack that navigates the intricate dance of love, loss, and self-discovery. The author invites you into his world, where heartfelt verses are a testament to his journey. He grapples with the absence of a father he never knew while finding guidance in his spiritual legacy. He confronts past mistakes and addiction, offering a profound apology to his mother that resonates with raw honesty. The collection delves deep into the tumultuous landscape of romantic love—from the dizzying highs of a "flawless" romance to the agonizing lows of a broken heart. Through poems that are both vulnerable and resilient, the author explores the challenges of trusting again and the hope that persists even after disappointment. Sucker4love Too is more than just poetry; it's a powerful narrative of resilience, a tribute to the enduring power of love, and a beacon for anyone seeking to find their way back to themselves.

Psalms in My Palms is a collection of heartfelt psalms, prayers, and poetic reflections born out of seasons of pain, redemption, and unshakable faith. Drawing from his personal journey through hardship, incarceration, and spiritual renewal, Coolgmack—offers words that meet readers in their darkest valleys and guide them toward God's light. Each piece blends lyrical beauty with scriptural truth, speaking to those who feel broken, oppressed, or forgotten. Within these pages are declarations of gratitude, prayers for strength and deliverance, and poetic portraits of God's unchanging love.

More than a book of poems, this is a devotional companion—a sacred space where you can pause, reflect, and write your own prayers in response. Psalms in My Palms is for anyone longing to be reminded that they are seen, chosen, and never alone. Whether rejoicing on the mountaintop or enduring a storm, you'll find words here to anchor your heart and lift your spirit.

Chronicles of a Hangry Black Soul is a raw, unapologetic poetry collection documenting a life hungry for truth, justice, and spiritual liberation. Through unfiltered verses, the author confronts systemic injustice, personal struggle, and the journey toward healing.The collection explores: **Social & Spiritual Commentary**: Exposing a "rigged" world of scams and fake love while offering a mirror for self-discovery and a guide through modern chaos. **The Prison System**: Raw testimony of dehumanization and isolation, where freedom is elusive and the system reduces public defenders to jokes.**Relationships & Loyalty**: Examining betrayal by fair-weather friends and celebrating the "Day Ones" who remained loyal through adversity. **Healing & Transformation**: Chronicling evolution from the "drug game" to "Elevation Season"—rising spiritually, mentally, and financially to build a new kingdom with divine wisdom.

Sucker4drugs chronicles the journey through addiction, despair, and recovery, exploring substance abuse, violence, incarceration, and redemption through raw street experiences. The **Destructive Cycle** Early poems depict the devastating effects of drug use, particularly PCP. Characters like "Dirty Diana" and "Derek" illustrate addiction's physical and emotional toll—paranoia, violence, incarceration, and betrayal..**Personal Struggle** Poems delve into loneliness, desperation, and internal conflict, portraying the relentless grip drugs have on mind and spirit. Recovery **and Hope** Amidst darkness, the collection offers messages of hope, encouraging honesty, faith, and spiritual growth as tools for healing. The **Healing Journey** The "Day One" through "Day 28" series intimately documents recovery's daily struggles—confronting temptation, rebuilding life, and finding resilience.

Identity and Purpose Poems explore self-discovery and reclaiming purpose, emphasizing that circumstances refine rather than define us.

They say love doesn't cost a thing—but for him, it costs everything. Sucker4Pain is a gritty, uncut testimony from a man who gave his all to the wrong women and nearly lost himself in the process. This ain't no love story—it's a survival story. Its raw pain served cold, dressed in designer lies and false promises. Through a poetic fusion of heartbreak, prison reflections, betrayal, addiction, and faith, this powerful collection gives voice to everyone who's ever been played, betrayed, locked up, or left behind. Told in vivid street verses and emotional confessionals, this book is more than poetry—it's a purge. A spiritual detox from toxic love and generational curses. From being set up and stripped down, to finding strength in the ruins, Sucker4Pain captures the real-life struggle of trusting the wrong women and finding God on the other side of grief.If you've ever been hurt, hustled, or hardened by love—you'll feel this in your soul.

Sucker4Lust is a collection of erotic poetry that delves into the raw, uninhibited world of desire and passion. The book is a journey through lust, presented through two distinct perspectives—that of a young, confident man consumed by his hunger, and women drawn to his intense charisma. The poems, which are at times witty, provocative, and tender, follow a narrative arc. They begin with an introduction to a world where lust is not a sin but a form of salvation. The stories then unfold through the eyes of a character known as "Mr. Thriller," a seductive and unapologetic figure who navigates his desires with a captivating swagger. His verses are direct and sensual, celebrating the thrill of a physical connection. The collection also includes a female point of view, exploring the intoxicating pull of this "magnetic space" and the surrender to a "willing death" of passion. The book concludes with an "Aftermath" section, where the focus shifts from a purely physical connection to a deeper, more lasting bond, suggesting that lust, when fully explored, can evolve into something more profound. Ultimately, Sucker 4 Lust is a poetic exploration of the body's truth and the soul's temptation.

This unique collection of poetry is a walk in the world of SlowMotion.the author/poet Relatable situations. Loving words. Takes you to a place of a hurting heart, overcoming pain. Bravery and boldness to rebuild. Poems about Mending Hearts. Coming together and finding understanding.I'm excited for the world to read my words.I want to show the world that it is possible to live out your wonderful dreams positively. Keep dreaming Big

..This unique collection of poetry is a walk in the world of SlowMotion.Relatable situations.Loving words. Takes you to a place of a hurting heart, overcoming pain. Bravery and boldness to rebuild. Poems about Mending Hearts. Coming together and finding understanding